Dear Parent:
Your child's love of reading starts here!

Every child learns to read in a different way and at his or her own speed. Some go back and forth between reading levels and read favorite books again and again. Others read through each level in order. You can help your young reader improve and become more confident by encouraging his or her own interests and abilities. From books your child reads with you to the first books he or she reads alone, there are I Can Read Books for every stage of reading:

SHARED READING
Basic language, word repetition, and whimsical illustrations, ideal for sharing with your emergent reader

BEGINNING READING
Short sentences, familiar words, and simple concepts for children eager to read on their own

READING WITH HELP
Engaging stories, longer sentences, and language play for developing readers

READING ALONE
Complex plots, challenging vocabulary, and high-interest topics for the independent reader

ADVANCED READING
Short paragraphs, chapters, and exciting themes for the perfect bridge to chapter books

I Can Read Books have introduced children to the joy of reading since 1957. Featuring award-winning authors and illustrators and a fabulous cast of beloved characters, I Can Read Books set the standard for beginning readers.

A lifetime of discovery begins with the magical words "I Can Read!"

Visit www.icanread.com for information
on enriching your child's reading experience.

For Tully
—L.D.

To all the silent heroes who have sacrificed
their lives for the safety of others.
—C.E.

I Can Read Book® is a trademark of HarperCollins Publishers.

Library of Congress Control Number: 2017942893
ISBN 978-0-06-243245-2 (trade bdg.) — ISBN 978-0-06-243243-8 (pbk.)

Typography by Jeff Shake
17 18 19 20 21 SCP 10 9 8 7 6 5 4 3 2 1   ❖   First Edition

I Can Read!

BEGINNING 1 READING

I Want to Be a
Police Officer

by Laura Driscoll

illustrated by Catalina Echeverri

HARPER
An Imprint of HarperCollinsPublishers

I am learning
all about bike safety.

Officer Green checks my helmet.

"Looks good, Eva!" she says.

"Snug around your head.

The strap fits well.

You are ready to ride!"

Officer Green is in the bike tent
at Town Safety Day.

She already put
more air in my tires.

She put a bell
on my handlebars.

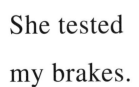

She tested
my brakes.

BRIIIING!

I know Officer Green from school.
Officer Green is at school
when we have fire drills.

I have seen Officer Green
all around town.
She makes me feel safe.

When I grow up,
I want to be just like her.

I see lots of police officers
at Town Safety Day.
One of them has a dog.

"I'm Officer Bell," he says.

"This is Gus."

Officer Bell and Gus

are in the K-9 unit.

Gus is a search-and-rescue dog.

"Gus uses his sense of smell
to find missing people,"
says Officer Bell.

I love animals.

Officer Bell is so lucky!

He gets to be a police officer

with a dog partner.

Another police officer

is making ID cards for kids.

She takes my photo

and my fingerprints.

She tells me, "It will be handy
for your parents to have
this ID card in an emergency."

The officer's name is Detective Lin.

"A detective?" I say.

"Do you solve mysteries?"

"Sort of," Detective Lin says.

"When a crime takes place,

I try to find out what happened.

I make a lot of phone calls.

I talk to a lot of people.

I ask a lot of questions."

19

I am good at asking questions.

Maybe I should be a detective!

SIT in a POLICE CAR!

Trooper Jones is talking to kids
about car safety.
He lets us sit in his police car!

Trooper Jones is a state trooper.

His job is to keep

roads and highways safe.

"I always wear my seatbelt,"
he says.
"It's a law that keeps us all safer.
I make sure drivers follow
all the rules of the road."

Hmm.

I am pretty good
at remembering rules.
I would probably be
a good state trooper.

TOWN SAFETY PLAY AREA

Officer Perez hands out flyers
about wilderness safety.
He is the game warden.

"Is that like a police officer
for the woods?" I ask.

"Yes!" says Officer Perez.

"I love working
in the great outdoors."

On the way home,

I see police officers in the parking lot.

They keep the traffic moving—

slowly but safely.

One officer stops the cars

so I can walk my bike

across the road.

It is Officer Green!

"Did you have fun
at Town Safety Day?"
Officer Green asks me.
"Yes!" I say.
"I did not know there were
so many ways to be a police officer."

Police officers work hard

to make every day

a safe day.

Meet the Police Officers

Patrol officer
a police officer whose job is to protect people and keep an area safe by making sure laws are followed

K-9 unit officer
a police officer who works as a team with a trained dog to find missing or hidden people or things

Police detective
a police officer who tries to find out all the facts about a crime

State trooper
a police officer who makes sure drivers follow traffic laws on highways and other roads

Game warden
a police officer who protects wildlife by making sure hunters and fishermen follow laws